COLLECTIVE BARGAINING IN THE PUBLIC SERVICE

Consulting Editor

ALBERT A. BLUM

MICHIGAN STATE UNIVERSITY

COLLECTIVE BARGAINING IN THE PUBLIC SERVICE

Edited by

DANIEL H. KRUGER/CHARLES T. SCHMIDT, Jr.

MICHIGAN STATE UNIVERSITY   UNIVERSITY OF RHODE ISLAND

RANDOM HOUSE · NEW YORK

Collective Bargaining in the Public Service: Kruger & Schmidt

FIRST PRINTING

Copyright © 1969 by Random House, Inc.
All rights reserved under International and Pan-American Copyright Conventions. Published in the United States by Random House, Inc., New York, and simultaneously in Canada by Random House of Canada Limited, Toronto.

Library of Congress Catalog Card Number: 69-19426

Manufactured in the United States of America by The Colonial Press Inc., Clinton, Mass.

PREFACE

Interest in collective bargaining in public employment has been growing since 1962, when President John F. Kennedy signed Executive Order 10988. This order marked a significant milestone in the history of public employment collective bargaining. Not only did it open the door to collective bargaining relationships for federal employees, but it stimulated the desire of other public employees at the state and local levels to negotiate with their employers. The appropriate state legislation or administrative action, or both, have been forthcoming, and as a result, since 1962 an increasing number of public employees, especially those employed in local governmental units, are being covered by labor agreements.

Collective bargaining in public employment represents an important development in employer-employee relations in the United States. Traditional relationships between the public employer and the public employee are being significantly altered as employee organizations that have obtained bargaining rights are sharing in the decision-making process on such matters as wages, hours, and conditions of employment. The sovereignty and authority of the public employer in personnel administration are being seriously challenged by collective bargaining. As public employees seek bargaining rights, the public employer is becoming ever more conscious of his personnel policies.

Collective bargaining in the public sector may also stimulate a growth of white-collar unionism in general. Further, such professional workers as teachers and nurses are engaging in collective bargaining through their associations, which are assuming functions hitherto performed by labor unions. An examination

v

of agreements negotiated by both professional associations and unions would show that they have many similarities. There are, however, differences, the most important of which is that professional associations seek to share in the decision-making process on matters relating to professional status. (This is also true of teacher's unions.)

In this volume of readings we attempt to highlight the experiences in public employment collective bargaining, limited as they may be. The readings focus on the nature of the emerging relationship between the parties, the importance of the legal framework, and reports that provide guidelines to a more effective implementation of public policy. Although public employment collective bargaining is taking place at all levels of government, readings have been selected to describe collective bargaining experiences at the federal and local levels. In addition, because of its importance, we have included a special case study of collective bargaining experiences in public education in Michigan.

Collective bargaining in public employment has raised important issues, both substantive and procedural. In a book of this size, we could deal only with those that, in our judgment, are the most important—namely, the resolution of impasses between the parties and the role of the state administrative agencies. To round out our review, we present a brief look at the future trends in this field as we see them. Finally, because the growth in public employment collective bargaining has stimulated interest and research in this subject, we have compiled a bibliography that lists selections from the growing body of pertinent literature in this field.

This book probably raises more questions than it answers. There are no simple answers to the complex problems of employers and employees—be they private or public—in living and working together. The relationships between the parties are dynamic, and there are no final and definitive answers. What is needed is an understanding of the forces that shape the collective bargaining process and the relationships between the parties. If this volume contributes to such an understanding, it will indeed serve a useful purpose.

We gratefully acknowledge the cooperation of the authors and